T0365460

To order additional copies of this book, contact
Toll Free +65 3165 7531 (Singapore)
Toll Free +60 3 3099 4412 (Malaysia)
www.partridgepublishing.com/singapore
orders.singapore@partridgepublishing.com

Book Illustrators: Lidya Riana and Roopal Jian (Front Cover Only)
Book Editor: Kim Lee

ISBN
ISBN: 978-1-5437-8238-7 (sc)
ISBN: 978-1-5437-8237-0 (e)

Print information available on the last page.

08/13/2024

PARTRIDGE

Preface

I have written Katy's Science Adventures Books 1 & 2 as Covid-19 Projects. They became creative ways to spend time with my granddaughters, Kate, and Christy. The projects revealed that we can still go global amidst border closures with technology as an enabler.

2024 sees the world living in an endemic COVID-19 state. It is also Nuclei Brand Marketing Solutions' 10th Anniversary. In celebration, I dedicate Katy's Science Adventures Book 3 to children of the world. As of 2020, Singapore's upper primary school children undergo computational and coding classes with greater emphasis placed on robotics and machine learning as the country moves into a digital economy. The Ministry of Education also focuses on nurturing stewards of the environment focusing on the value of sustainability and the importance of the practices of reuse, reduce and recycle.

I had the opportunity to attend a course at the National University of Singapore Business School on Sustainability — The Next Challenge. It has provided me with a good overview of the broad range of issues and challenges in business sustainability and built awareness on context and applications of sustainability in environmental, social, and governmental arenas. The course equipped me with key skills that are relevant in helping my clients to advance sustainability in their organisations.

Pedagogy is the science of education. The inquiry-based approach is an engaging and effective means of introducing science to children.

Science is about everything around us. Children are naturally curious. In this book, I am pleased to introduce Ann, Katy's younger sister, a fellow young scientist. Katy and Ann like to explore and discover things. Science provides them with appropriate, fun-filled experiences to whet their appetite for learning. Their parents, grandparents and friends can also join in the fun. **Science** is also critical to the improvement of children's observation, reading, writing, and reasoning skills. Book 3 aims at fostering greater awareness of technological changes and promote sustainable living by empowering children to play their part towards achieving a greener tomorrow.

Coding

Coding with Scratch is elementary.
Ready-made blocks make easy entry.
Sprite builds a script-block.
Press a green flag to move the sprite-block,
And coding will unlock.

What is Science?

Science is about discovering the world around us through observing, asking, listening, describing, and experimenting. It encourages us to be curious and teaches us about the diversity of both Living Things and Non-Living Things.

Diversity

Different types of things around us

Living things

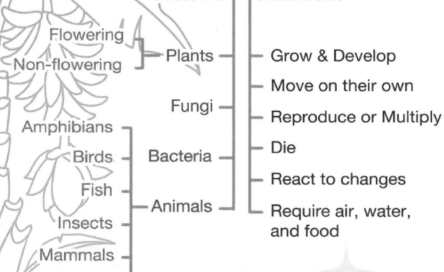

divided into | characteristics

Flowering
Non-flowering ⎤ Plants

Fungi

Amphibians
Birds
Fish
Insects
Mammals
Reptiles ⎦ Animals

Bacteria

- Grow & Develop
- Move on their own
- Reproduce or Multiply
- Die
- React to changes
- Require air, water, and food

Ceramic
Igneous
Rock
Metals ⎦ Ground

Glass
Plastic
Steel ⎦ Man Made

Cotton
Rubber
Wood ⎦ Plants

Cowhide
Silk
Wool ⎦ Animals

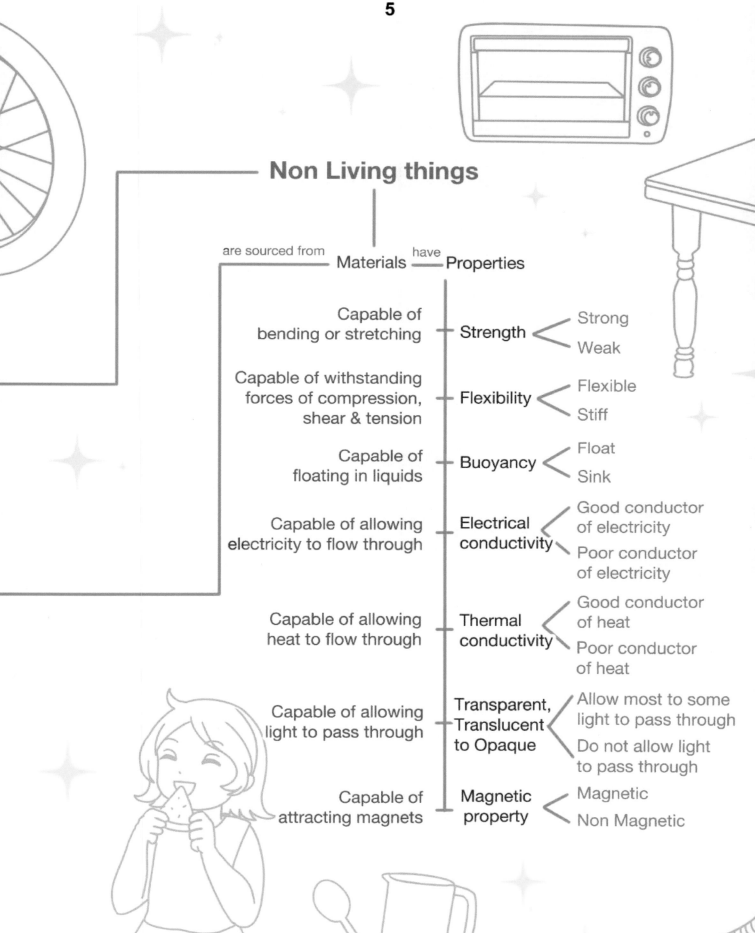

Non Living things

are sourced from — Materials — have Properties

Capable of bending or stretching	Strength	Strong / Weak
Capable of withstanding forces of compression, shear & tension	Flexibility	Flexible / Stiff
Capable of floating in liquids	Buoyancy	Float / Sink
Capable of allowing electricity to flow through	Electrical conductivity	Good conductor of electricity / Poor conductor of electricity
Capable of allowing heat to flow through	Thermal conductivity	Good conductor of heat / Poor conductor of heat
Capable of allowing light to pass through	Transparent, Translucent to Opaque	Allow most to some light to pass through / Do not allow light to pass through
Capable of attracting magnets	Magnetic property	Magnetic / Non Magnetic

ADVENTURES WITH LIVING THINGS

Just no spicy food please!!!

Three years after the Covid-19 pandemic, Katy's parents organise a dinner with some friends in celebration of the new normal. Katy's grandfather has prepared his famous chilli crabs, and her grandmother has prepared the popular Singapore chicken rice dish.

The dinner table is beautifully laid. Katy spots her grandfather's giant bowl of red-hot chilli crabs and decides to try a spoonful of the chilli crab sauce. Immediately, Katy feels like her mouth is on fire!

Just then, Ann walks into the dining room. She sees her sister, Katy, fanning her mouth frantically with her hands.

Ann is alarmed. She spots a jar of ice-cold blue pea tea and hands the pot to her. Katy quickly gulps down a cup of tea. She feels as though steam is coming out of her ears and heaves a sigh of relief.

Her grandfather looks at Katy in dismay. He tells them that today's chilli crab sauce is extra spicy. Katy's grandfather has used the extra hot chilli padi that is growing in his garden.

When their guests arrive, Katy scoops a huge ladleful of chicken rice onto her plate and declares, "No more spicy food, please!" Everyone laughs.

FUN FACTS

Food, glorious food!
Let's grow vegetables at home!

Katy's and Ann's grandfather loves gardening.
He has "green fingers," meaning that he is good at gardening!
The National Parks Board (NParks) of Singapore launched an initiative
in 2020 to encourage people to grow produce at home by distributing
free packets of leafy fruit and vegetable seeds. Called "Gardening
with Edibles," this initiative supports Singapore's "30 by 30" goal to
produce 30 percent of its nutritional needs by the year 2030.

Cucumber from the garden

Bitter Gourd from the garden

To the bowl for achar or pickled vegetables

To the table - yummy bitter gourd omelette

Water Spinach from the garden

Lovely Tomatoes for salad.

Ready to be pan-fried with garlic.

Ladies' finger or Okra for curry

Seed Vending Machine.

Grandfather is delighted to get these seeds.
He has created vegetable plots in his garden and
enthusiastically planted cucumber, bitter gourd,
ladies' finger, and chilli seeds. He gleefully harvests
these vegetables. They are grown organically,
without using poisons to kill weeds or insects.
The vegetables go from the garden to the
frying pan, to the plate. Katy and her family
can taste the freshness in every mouthful!
With today's technology, vending machines
can dispense packs of seeds for gardeners!

Experiment E1
Make your own special tea!

Katy and Ann think it will be great to use some of the plants in the garden, like blue-pea, ginger, and lemon grass, to make beverages to go with vegetable dishes.

1 The Blue-pea Flower Tea

Katy and Ann place blue-pea flowers in a jar and infuse them in hot water.

This makes a beautiful blue and lightly scented drink. The blue-pea flower tea is truly refreshing.

Katy tells Ann they can have more fun by changing the colour of the blue-pea drink. Katy adds a little lemon juice. The acidic juice turns the blue tea purple!

2 Lemon grass and ginger tea

Katy and Ann bash 3 stalks of lemon grass using a mortar and pestle, then put them into a pot of boiling water.

They add 4 slices of ginger and 2 tablespoons of palm sugar or brown sugar. The drink they create is simply delicious.

FUN FACTS

Grow vegetables without watering them, and rear fish without changing water!

Katy has an idea for a new adventure. She wants to build a mini-aquaponics system. She has learnt that aquaponics, on a big scale, blends aquaculture with soil-less farming. It is a new form of agriculture, but it can be scaled down and done at home!

Katy goes online to search for the things she needs to build such a system at home. She plans to grow some basil and keep small fish.

The aquaponics system creates a circuit for fish, vegetables, and micro-organisms in a closed environment. Fish poop is broken down and decomposed by micro-organisms that also turn the stinky ammonia gas given off into nutrients. These nutrients then feed the plants. As the plants absorb the nutrients, the water is cleaned, and the fish are kept alive. Microorganisms, fish, and plants all depend on each other to thrive.

Katy asks her sister, Ann, to join her in this new adventure. The girls go online and buy some net pot baskets with collar sponges, hydroponic clay pebbles, and basil seeds to plant. They also get 3 fish and name the fishes in their experiment Blossom, Cotton, and Merely.

The Accidental Rescue!

As part of nurturing stewards of the environment, Katy's and Ann's school campus has created sustainability features, like the Eco Pond. Katy and Ann love to sit and read by this Eco Pond. It's designed by Aunty Bee 🐝 ,a family friend and former student of the school. The Eco Pond system always has crystal clear water. It also has fish like koi swimming in it.

On one occasion the girls, together with their schoolmates Lulu and Laurie, notice a small fluffy brown ball amongst the roots of a tree near the Eco Pond. Katy had to look hard as it was well camouflaged against its roots. She gently scooped up the fluffy ball into her hands. It is a baby bird, and Katy can feel the frightened creature trembling.

At that moment, Katy and Ann hear some noise from behind. They look back and spot a hornbill perched on a branch of the tree. The hornbill looks mean, and it is staring at the fluffy brown ball in Katy's palms!

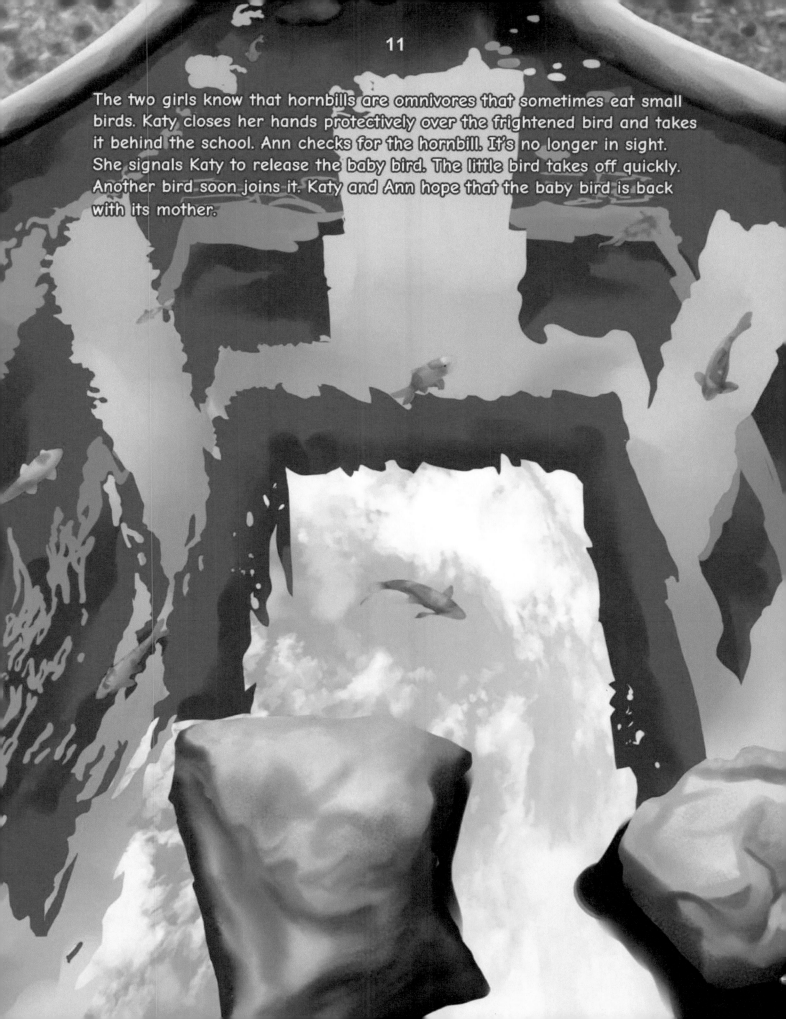

The two girls know that hornbills are omnivores that sometimes eat small birds. Katy closes her hands protectively over the frightened bird and takes it behind the school. Ann checks for the hornbill. It's no longer in sight. She signals Katy to release the baby bird. The little bird takes off quickly. Another bird soon joins it. Katy and Ann hope that the baby bird is back with its mother.

The girls see their other friends Clara and Lottie nearby and excitedly share the tale of their accidental rescue. Katy even shares the picture that Ann took with her iPad of the little bird resting on the palms of her hands.

Experiment E2
How to make an aquaponic system

What you need from a local "dollar" or online store

1) A large glass jar with a mouth 3 inches or 7.6 centimetres in diameter.
2) A 3-inch or 7.6-centimetre net planter or pot.
3) Hydroponic clay pebbles
4) A fish, like a guppy, goldfish, minnow or Siamese fighting fish
5) Aquarium water – a small pail of tap water that has been left standing for 2 days.
6) Plants, e.g., Coriander, basil.

1 Fill the jar with aquarium water. Leave an inch or 2.5cm of air space at the top of the jar for the roots and fish to breathe.

2 Add the fish into the glass jar.

3 Add the plants, fully submerging their roots in the water.

Plant

Net Planter

2.5 cm air space

Roots in the water

Sunlight

Clay pebbles

Fish

4 Place the assembled aquaponics system in a place where it can get sunlight in the day.

5 Feed your fish twice a day with fish food.

6 Top up the water as needed to keep the plant roots submerged.

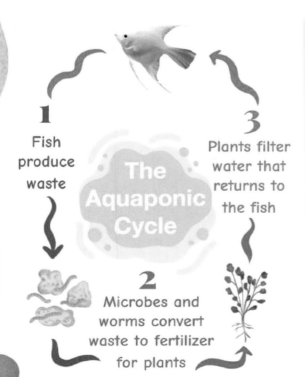

1 Fish produce waste

The Aquaponic Cycle

2 Microbes and worms convert waste to fertilizer for plants

3 Plants filter water that returns to the fish

OBSERVATION & CONCLUSION

1) The fish waste builds up within days. You can smell the stinky ammonia when the water becomes dirty and cloudy.
2) The hydroponic clay pebbles act as biological filters or biofilters to help clean the dirty water and turn ammonia from poop to nutrients (nitrates) for the plants.
3) The plants grow well. The leaves can be used for garnishing food. The closed loop system in aquaponics helps to keep the water clean. What is waste from one organism, the fish, becomes food for another organism, the plant.
Nothing is wasted.

Do you know?
What is high-tech agri-food?

The world went into panic-buying frenzies with the COVID-19 pandemic. As more nations went into lockdown, food supplies were disrupted. People in big cities needed food, but food could not be sent to them. It is important to be ready for the future by protecting both our water and food supplies. Agriculture is the business of producing food on farms. High-tech agriculture of food uses new technology to grow food more efficiently. What can hi-tech agri-food look like? For one, instead of growing vegetables flat on fields outdoors, they can be grown upwards and indoors in innovative vertical farming systems. This makes it easier to grow more vegetables in small urban spaces, and without using pesticides. High-tech agri-food is one way to produce more food locally and boost food security, which is the aim of Singapore's "30 by 30" goal. "30 by 30" is supported by the new Agri-Food Cluster Transformation Fund, which has devoted S$60 million to the mission, reported The Straits Times newspaper. Besides edible crops, organisations are developing high-tech fish farms to grow fish safely in a scientifically controlled environment.

Urban Fish Farming in a Container

Jade Perch

Red Snapper

Barramundi

The Straits Times reported on Singapore's first urban fish farm in shipping containers. This high-tech aquaculture system was launched on 19th November 2023. It is part of an initiative to support local urban farmers. Fish tanks for raising jade perch are housed inside shipping containers. The fish will be sold in markets when they reach 500g to 600g in weight. Other species of fish can also be farmed in such a recirculating aquaculture system, which can raise a great number of fish in small spaces under controlled temperature, water quality, light and other environmental conditions.

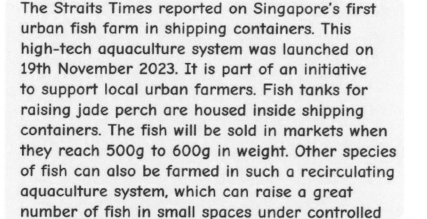

Fish tank inside the container

Going Bananas!

Katy and Ann are spending their June holidays in Kuala Lumpur, the capital of Malaysia. They enjoy playing with their Malaysian friends and relatives. Katy and Ann tour the Petrosains Discovery Centre at the KLCC Mall and spend time looking for a birthday present that they are sharing to buy for Satish, their friend and hobby enthusiast, at the LEGO® store.

The highlight of the trip is a private excursion to a banana and ornamental plant farm at Tanjong Malim. The owners of the farm are family acquaintances. They are tissue culture and horticulture experts in growing plants. Aunty Ling is an exceptionally good guide.

At the start of the tour, Katy, Ann, and their parents peer curiously through the glass windows of the laboratory where bananas are micro propagated by tissue culture. Tissue culture allows the propagation of masses of disease-free plants.

The farm supplies banana plantlets to palm oil plantations. The banana plants are suitable for growing alongside rows of oil palm trees. Integrating them like this into an oil palm plantation creates an intercropping system.

The integration of crops makes the most of land use, increases what the land can produce, and creates additional income for the oil palm growers. The 15-acre farm and its produce are impressive. Aunty Ling surprises everyone with a box containing banana and ornamental plantlets. Katy's grandfather is so thrilled with the gift, he starts to daydream about planting the banana plantlet and the harvest of bananas it will give. Everyone thanked Aunty Ling for a fruitful day!

Types of plants and how they reproduce

There are flowering and non-flowering plants. Non-flowering plants do not bear flowers or fruits. To grow, three different kinds of plant parts interact with the surroundings to get water and nutrients to make food. These plant parts are the roots, stems, and leaves. Plant roots like to grow underground and towards water, while a plant's stem bears leaves that grow towards sunlight.

1 Roots hold plants in the soil. They also bring water and nutrients from the soil into the plants.

2 Stems hold plants up above the ground, help the leaves reach sunlight and carry water and food throughout the plants.

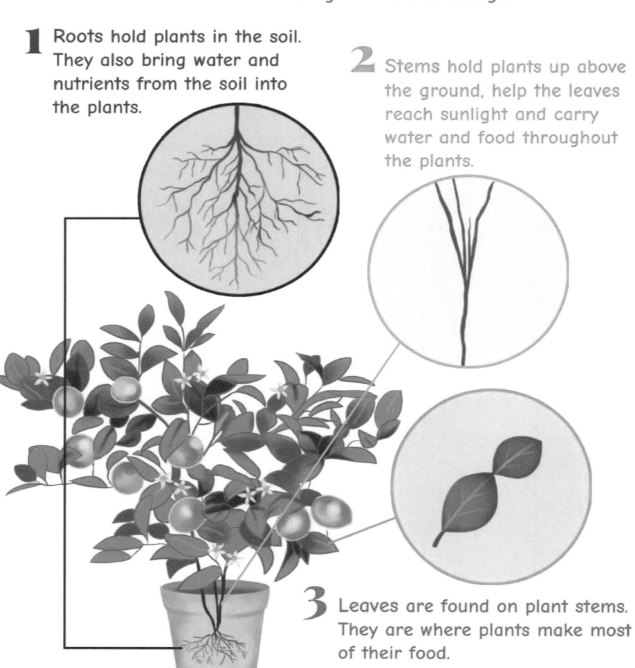

3 Leaves are found on plant stems. They are where plants make most of their food.

Another three different plant parts help to grow new plants. These are flowers, fruits, and seeds.

4 Flowers grow at the end of stems. They are often the most colourful part of the plants. These colours attract insects like bees and butterflies to pollinate the flowers. After pollination, flowers make fruits and seeds.

5 Fruits develop from flowers. Like flowers, fruits come in a variety of colours, shapes and sizes. Most fruits are edible. Many are sweet, tasty, and fleshy, but some can be poisonous. Fruits can be carried away from the plant by water, animals, and wind. Why? Because they contain seeds that need to find a new place to grow.

6 Seeds are important for growing new plants. This is called reproduction.

A fruit can have one seed or many, depending on the kind of plant. For example, the mango fruit contains just one seed, but an orange contains many seeds. Some fruits can split open explosively, tossing seeds away from the plant, so that the seeds may find new space to grow in.

Do you know?
What is photosynthesis?

The chlorophyll that gives leaves their green colour uses sunlight to make sugar that the plant uses for food. In doing so, oxygen is released into the air. This process of making food from light is called photosynthesis.

In the day, plants take in carbon dioxide gas through their leaves and release oxygen through photosynthesis.

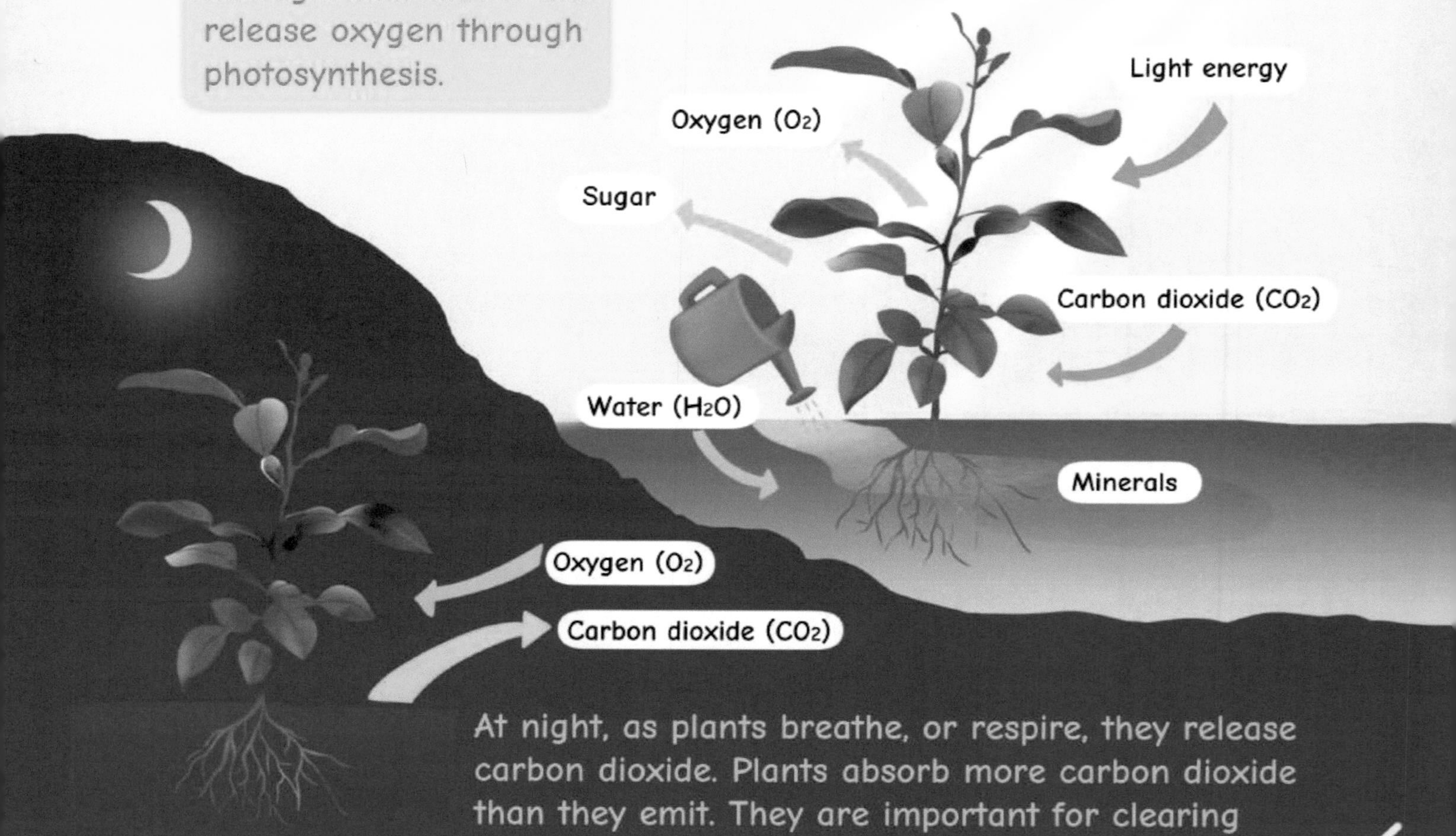

Oxygen (O_2)

Sugar

Light energy

Carbon dioxide (CO_2)

Water (H_2O)

Minerals

Oxygen (O_2)

Carbon dioxide (CO_2)

At night, as plants breathe, or respire, they release carbon dioxide. Plants absorb more carbon dioxide than they emit. They are important for clearing carbon dioxide from the air.

Leafy green vegetables are rich in chlorophyll. They are also a healthy food choice for people. They play a part in a balanced diet, supporting a healthy weight and healthy body composition of muscle and fat.

Do you know?

The Greenhouse Effect

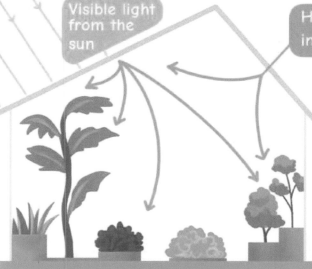

Sun's rays

Visible light from the sun

Heat from plants in the greenhouse

A greenhouse isn't green! It's a house with roof and walls made of glass. Greenhouses are used to grow plants. They receive sunlight and heat through the glass in the day, and stay warm at night, even in winter because of the heat trapped in the greenhouse.

The earth is surrounded by a layer of gases called the atmosphere. The atmosphere acts like a greenhouse. Sunlight passes through it like the glass of a green house. When sunlight reaches the earth, some of it is reflected into space, but some remain in the atmosphere. Infra-red (IR) rays are part of sunlight. These rays warm the atmosphere, causing temperatures to rise. Gases like carbon dioxide, methane, water vapour, nitrous oxide, and synthetic fluorinated gases trap heat. They are called greenhouse gases because they make the planet hotter. This is known as the Greenhouse Effect. Some human activities like agriculture and burning fossil fuels, also create greenhouse gases. Like a glass greenhouse, Earth's greenhouse is full of plants that can help to balance the Greenhouse Effect.

CO_2 and other gases in the atmosphere trap heat, keeping the earth warm

Atmosphere

Some sunlight that hits the earth is reflected back into space. Some becomes heat trapped in the atmosphere

What The Fish!

Katy, Ann, and their parents enjoy their holidays in Sydney visiting friends and relatives. They love picnics at Bondi Beach. Apart from the sandy beach, beautiful sunshine and sound of the waves, the girls enjoy walking on the beach, watching surfers riding the waves, and lovely meals at many of the nearby eateries.

Katy and Ann also like to build sandcastles with their spades and pails. They can sometimes spot tiny sea creatures and look for shells to add to their collections back home in Singapore. Ann is merrily looking for shells. Suddenly, she stops and swallows hard. Ann has been reading about the Portuguese-man-of-war jellyfish and it looks as if she has found one at the tip of her spade!

Bluebottle Jellyfish

She yells for Daddy and Katy to come look. Daddy sees that Ann is upset and very scared. He tells the two girls to end their day at the beach. They hurriedly pack all their plastic sandcastle building tools and beach mat, and leave the beach as fast as they can.

The Portuguese-man-of-war is covered with venom-filled cells called nematocysts that can shoot out a sting and paralyse small creatures. For humans, their sting is excruciatingly painful but not deadly.

Katy's mother is having coffee with Aunty MJ and Uncle C at a café near the beach. The frightened Ann tells Mummy about their find. They listen to her breathlessly describing their close encounter. Upon researching, the girls believe that it's likely they have found a more common Bluebottle jellyfish, which is smaller and less poisonous than the Portuguese-man-of-war. However, its sting can still cause intense pain and sores where it touches the skin. Aunty MJ is glad that Katy and Ann stayed away from the creature.

It's concerning that scientists have found climate change affects ecosystems in various ways, including altering ocean temperatures and acidity, which can impact jellyfish populations. Scientists also say that global warming increases the jellyfish population because they love warm waters. This can make them a nuisance in summer.

Woof
Woof

Do you know?

What is Global Warming?

Global warming refers to climate change. This is happening because the average temperature on earth is rising as increasing levels of greenhouse gases, like carbon dioxide, methane, and water vapour, warm the planet. The ice in the North and South poles is melting under this heat. This is causing sea levels to rise. Global warming also causes droughts and floods that can destroy crops.

We need to reduce environmentally unfriendly activities to reduce global warming and the impact of climate change. Here are some things that contribute to global warming.

Burning of fossil fuels in manufacturing and transportation

Deforestation

Construction of concrete buildings, roadways etc

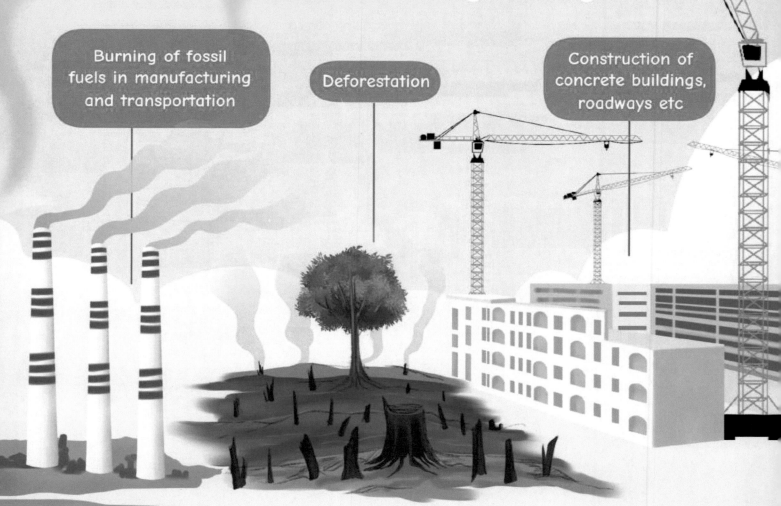

FUN FACTS

Katy shares the 3Rs of the environment

Reduce   **Reuse**   **Recycle**

Here are some ways to reduce waste

We can play our part to save Mother Earth by reducing the use of plastics. We can use our own water bottle at water dispensers or use bamboo toothbrushes instead of disposable plastic ones.

We can keep reusable bags handy when we are shopping for groceries.

We can donate used clothes, reuse used paper for note paper, etc.

We can recycle packaging materials, old newspaper, letters and envelopes, cans/tins, plastic bottles etc.

We can also separate our garbage, for example, wet from dry, or plastics from glass. We can dispose of recyclable materials like cardboard cartons, coffee capsules, plastic bags, or containers, by placing them in appropriate bins at designated recycling collection areas.

Let's Go Green!

Mummy has a brilliant idea for Katy's 11th birthday party. It's an eco-friendly party! Mummy has ordered Katy's favourite pesto pasta and simply mushroom pizza for lunch. Katy and Ann are busy helping mummy prepare goody bags for their friends. Each of them is getting a reusable goody bag with Mummy's delicious oatmeal cookies and blueberry muffins packed in a reusable lunch box, and orange juice in a recycled bottle.

Katy has invited their neighbours, Satish, Sumitar, Nahar, Matt and Justin to the celebration. The children are excited. Katy's and Ann's Mummy has a surprise for all of them. She has planned activities for the entire day starting with an Urban Farm Tour at 9 a.m. This is part of the Go Green SG programme. Go Green SG is a whole-of-nation movement for everyone of us to work together to make Singapore a green, liveable, and climate-resilient country. More than 100 organisations have come forward to create more than 250 events and activities. They include learning journeys, workshops and sustainability tours like the Urban Farm Tour.

After enjoying the morning farm excursion and a delicious birthday lunch, everyone gets to make their own mini terrarium garden to bring home. Mummy has gotten the children all the materials they need for this activity. Katy's grandfather is the judge for the best designed terrarium. Everyone is having such fun creating their own terrarium. Matt's terrarium wins! Katy's grandfather places big blue ribbon next to it. Matt also gets a box of chocolates as first prize.

Experiment E3

Make your own mini terrarium garden

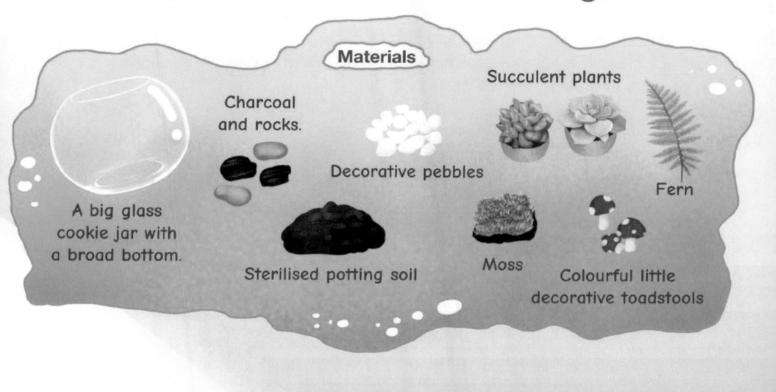

Materials

Charcoal and rocks.

Decorative pebbles

Succulent plants

Fern

A big glass cookie jar with a broad bottom.

Sterilised potting soil

Moss

Colourful little decorative toadstools

A terrarium has its own mini climate. It can hold warmth and moisture, just like the earth's atmosphere or a greenhouse. Sunlight enter through the glass, and warms up the terrarium just like it does the earth through its atmosphere.

The Amazing Water Story!

Katy and Ann are delighted to have Uncle Gid visit. He is a good friend of their parents. Uncle Gid travels all over the world and has many interesting stories to share. He tells the girls about his recent trip to a leachate water treatment plant in Asia. Leachate is a waste liquid formed when landfill waste decomposes and rainwater filters through the waste and picks up toxins.

The girls have read that the world produces more than two billion tonnes of solid waste every year, and this is likely to increase by 2050 as the world's population grows. Much of the waste ends up in landfills.

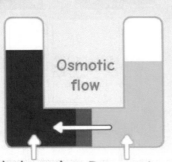

Osmotic flow

Leachate water   Pure water

Pressure

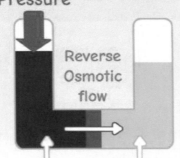

Reverse Osmotic flow

Leachate water   Pure water

Landfill Bin

Reverse Osmosis is a technology commonly used to treat leachate. It purifies leachate by using high pressure to force the liquid against a special filter called a membrane. This pressure allows pure water through the membrane and keeps contaminants like large particles and toxins out.

Experiment E4
How to clean dirty water?

By mechanical filtration

1 Get an empty litre bottle. Carefully cut it in half. Turn the mouth of the bottle upside down into the cut-off bottom half of the bottle.

2 Place some cotton wool at the mouth of bottle.

3 Add a layer of sand.

4 Add a layer of broken charcoal chips.

6 Add a layer of larger stones.

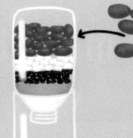

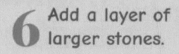

5 Add another layer of gravel or pebbles.

7 Pour in some dirty water and see what collects at the base of the bottle.

! NB: Charcoal absorbs contaminants and impurities.

By chemical purification using alum

1 Put some soil in a litre of water in a plastic bottle. Stir till the water turns murky or muddy.

Water →

Soil →

Aluminum Sulphate

Flocs

2 Add 1/2 teaspoon of alum shavings* (aluminium sulphate). Alum acts as a coagulant, pulling smaller particles to stick to it. This eventually forms larger heavier particles that settle at the bottom.

3 Stir well and let the water stand for 6 hours.

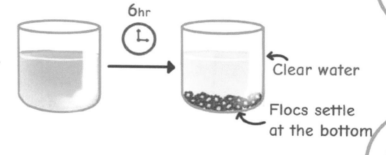

6hr

Clear water

Flocs settle at the bottom

4 Remove the larger particles by pouring the treated water through a coffee filter.

NB: You can buy an alum bar on-line and use a craft pen knife to scrape alum shavings off it.

ADVENTURES WITH NON-LIVING THINGS

A turn too far!

Katy and Ann are at their neighbour's house. They see Nahar and Satish struggling to open a bottle at the kitchen table. The boys keep their pet spiders in the bottle, and they cannot open the screw-on lid. Someone has twisted the lid on too tightly. Nahar and Satish are panicking as the spiders have been in the jar for two days and the creatures are not moving. The boys are not sure how much air is left in the jar or if the spiders are dead. Nahar tries to turn the lid with all his might. Suddenly, he screams. The children see that Nahar's thumb is strangely bent at a joint. Ann calls out to Nahar's mother for help, and she hurries to take him to the nearest clinic.

Meanwhile, Katy asks for a lid opener. Satish finds the gadget in the kitchen drawer. It turns the lid open quickly and easily. This gadget is a simple machine. The spiders start to crawl again. They are alive! Now, the children wait patiently in the house for Nahar to return. Poor Nahar comes home with his thumb in a brace. Nahar's mother tells the children that when they are in trouble, they need to ask for help from the adults.

Fun Facts on SIMPLE MACHINES

Simple machines like the gadget that unscrewed the bottle cap help us to do the job with less effort and energy. Examples of simple machines found in everyday life are:

1 Ladders and staircases. These are slopes called inclined planes. If the slant of the inclined plane is gentle, little effort is needed to move a load or object up the slope. If the slope is steep, it takes more effort.

2 Window blinds. A pulley is a wheel with a groove that has a rope or belt running in it. Pulleys help lift a load or object vertically. You use pulleys to raise or lower window blinds.

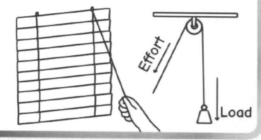

3 The doorknob is a simple machine involving a Wheel and Axle. The wheel and axle consists of a round wheel that works together with a stick-like axle. The doorknob acts as the wheel. Inside the knob there is an axle that moves the latch so that the door can open.

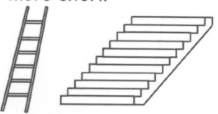

Axle   Wheel   Rotation

4 A seesaw, a stapler and a broom are simple machines involving levers. A lever amplifies effort applied to create a force to move a load

1. A seesaw is a 1st class lever. It has a fulcrum (f) in the middle, with effort (F) and load (L) on either side. Depending on where the fulcrum is, a small child can lift an adult.
2. A stapler is a 2nd class lever. The load (L) is between the fulcrum (f) and the effort (F).
3. A broom is a 3rd class lever. The top where it is held is the fulcrum (f), and effort (F) is applied between that and the load (L) on the floor.
4. A knife is a wedge which is used to seperate or cut objects.

5 A bicycle uses gears. Gears are toothed or pegged discs that interlock. As one gear is turned, it will turn the gear next to it in the opposite direction. Gears are used to move a bicycle.

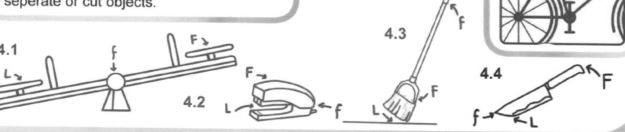

4.1   4.2   4.3   4.4

The "Marvel" of Quantum Physics

Ann is helping Katy declutter their playroom. They come across an Ant Oasis Science Kit and LEGO®ants that they built some time ago. Katy recalls the Marvel movies – Ant-man films, especially Ant-Man and the Wasp: Quantumania. This science fiction movie told a story using quantum science to explore how something can exist in more than one place at the same time. It also explored time travel. Katy really enjoyed the science in the movie and the fantastic possibilities it could create.

So, what is quantum science, also known as quantum physics? It is the study of the tiniest things — about atoms, molecules and sub-atomic particles like quarks, protons, neutrons, electrons, and how they interact with light, like photons. A photon is a package of light energy.

SOLAR CELL

ELECTRON MICROSCOPE

QUANTUM PHYSICS

Quantum science doesn't just exist in movies and textbooks. Quantum technology can be found in everyday life today. It first gave us the transistor, invented in 1947. The transistor paved the way for modern computers and digital communication. Other examples of technologies using quantum physics include lasers, solar cells, electron microscopes, and many more. Katy hopes to learn more as she ventures further into the study of science.

Do you know?
What is Artificial Intelligence (AI)?

Some things like animals, people, plants, air, and water come from nature. They are natural. No human made them.

Some things are man-made, like buildings, vehicles, aeroplanes, and drones. Man-made machines like the cake mixer, computer, car, vacuum cleaner, fan, and robot are said to be artificial (not created by nature).

Intelligence is about the ability to learn, reason and understand. Artificial Intelligence (AI) is a science that makes machines with the abilities to adapt, reason and provide solutions. AI creates systems that can function intelligently and independently. AI can "see" using cameras. It can learn by collecting data and processing the data to reason or make decisions. We call this machine learning. Machine learning programmes are called algorithms.

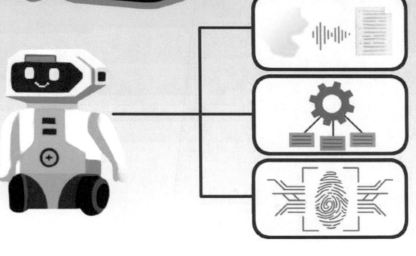

Speech Recognition

Natural Language Processing

Pattern Recognition

AI can "listen" and "speak." We call this speech recognition.
AI can read and write. We call this natural language processing.
AI can see patterns. We call this pattern recognition.

Ann's hand at Coding

Ann enjoys many fun screen-based projects at her coding school. She began her coding adventures there by learning to use Scratch to create computer games by piecing together different coloured blocks. She writes programmes for the different characters or objects called Sprites in her games.

Make a LEGO® set come to life!

The fun goes beyond the screen when Ann gets to visit her favourite LEGO® store. It's a special treat for her. Ann and her sister, Katy, love checking out LEGO® augmented reality (AR) app. It allows customers to use their creativity by mixing virtual and physical LEGO® play in new and fun ways. Children can play with digital versions of some of the most popular LEGO® sets. They can make racetracks materialise to launch and race LEGO® AR models in.

Ann's eyes gleam with excitement as she sees her parents pick up the LEGO® Robot R2D2 for payment at the cashier. She has been longing for this robot and she is getting it as a wonderful birthday present! Ann wears a big smile as she walks out of the shop. At home, Ann is eager to assemble the ROBOT R2D2 as soon as possible. She asks Katy to help her to build her robot. When the girls finished building it and successfully programmed it to move, Ann gleefully paraded the robot down the street. All her friends were envious of her new toy.

Do you know?
What is a robot?

A robot is a combination of a computer and a machine. Robots can help us to do work faster, better, more safely and automatically. They can even work in places where humans cannot be in, like deep underwater. Robots come in various kinds, sizes, and shapes. A robot has a camera to 'see.' It also has sensors that help it to know where it is, such as an ultrasonic sensor that can measure the distance of an object by using ultrasonic waves.

Coding is the computer language that gives machine instructions. Basically, there are two types of coding. There is visual block-based programming such as Scratch which children often start with. This form of coding has a visual set of commands and instructions which makes it easy to use. The other type of coding is text-based such as C, C++, Java, Javascript and Python. With the right code, or set of machine instructions, the robot can now act. When it is given movable mechanical parts, it can move when commanded by the computer, like an R2D2 robot.

So, a robot is a programmable machine that can do things. It has computer software that helps direct it. It can also act independently without human intervention.

A waiter robot

A cleaner robot

Robot vacuums

Experiment E5
Make an ART BOT – an Art Robot!

What happens when you add Art to the skills and concepts from STEM (Science, Technology, Engineering and Mathematics)? You get STEAM (Science, Technology, Engineering, Art and Mathematics). This can make exciting things happen. See how STEAM comes together in this colourful and fun experiment!

Materials you need:

A paper cup   A motor   A nut   Multipurpose glue

A 9-volt battery   Coloured pens   A switch

1 Put a drop of multipurpose glue on the nut and stick it onto the spindle of the motor.

Hole

2 Cut a hole at the top of the paper cup. Glue the motor into the hole with the wires at the top.

3 Glue 4 coloured pens onto the sides of the paper cup so that the cup can stand on the pens.

4 Glue the 9-volt battery horizontally next to the pens on top of the cup.

5 Connect the switch and battery to the motor. Your artbot is complete.

6 Place the art bot on a sheet of drawing paper, switch it on, and watch it create art!

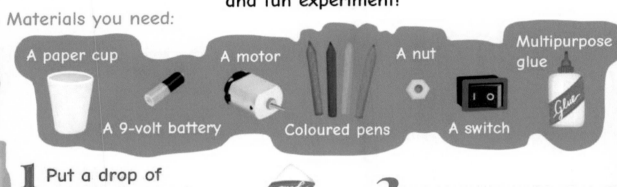

NOTES

Printed in the United States
by Baker & Taylor Publisher Services